# Unbelievable Pictures and Facts About Old English Sheepdogs

By: Olivia Greenwood

# Introduction

Old English Sheepdogs are big and furry dogs, who make wonderful companions. It sometimes looks like they can't see as their hair often grows over their eyes. Today we will be exploring the world of Old English Sheepdogs.

# Is this particular dog breed popular in America?

Many years old this breed was very popular in America. Today these dogs are moderately popular in America. There will always be people in America who are totally in love with this dog breed.

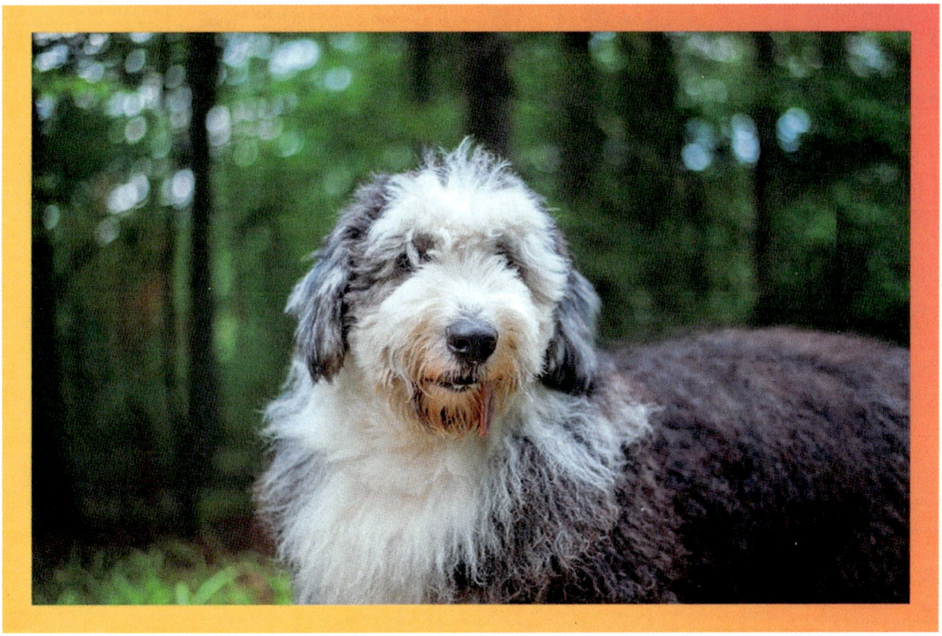

## What should families know before getting one of these dogs?

Firstly families who wish to own this dog breed need to know that they will require regular grooming. They also have a tendency to bump into things. If you have small children they can knock over your children by mistake without meaning to. This happens because of their herding instincts.

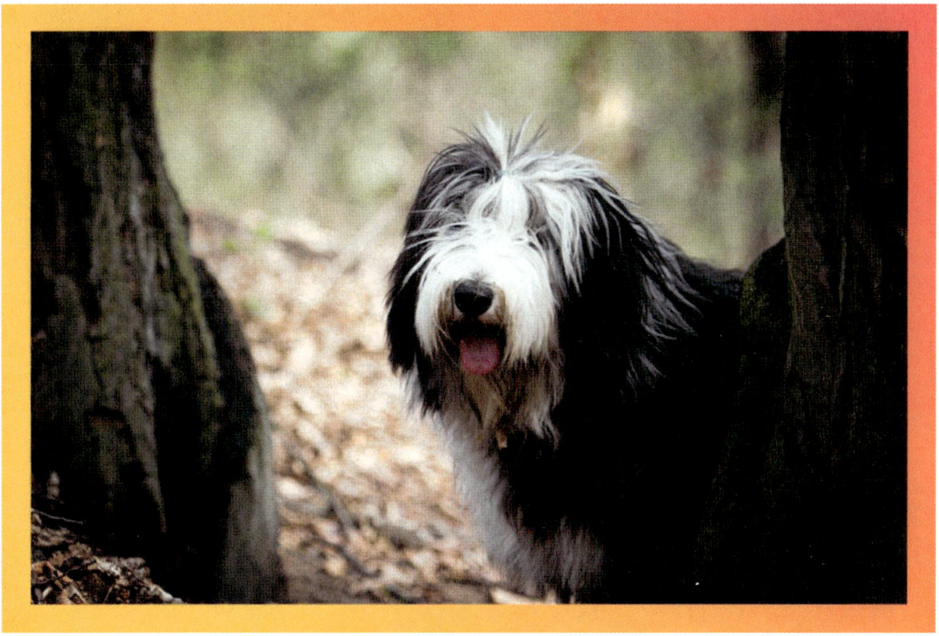

# Are these dogs any good at being security dogs?

The answer is a big no. These dogs are very playful, affectionate and friendly. They make terrible security dogs as they love everybody. They are not good at scaring people away.

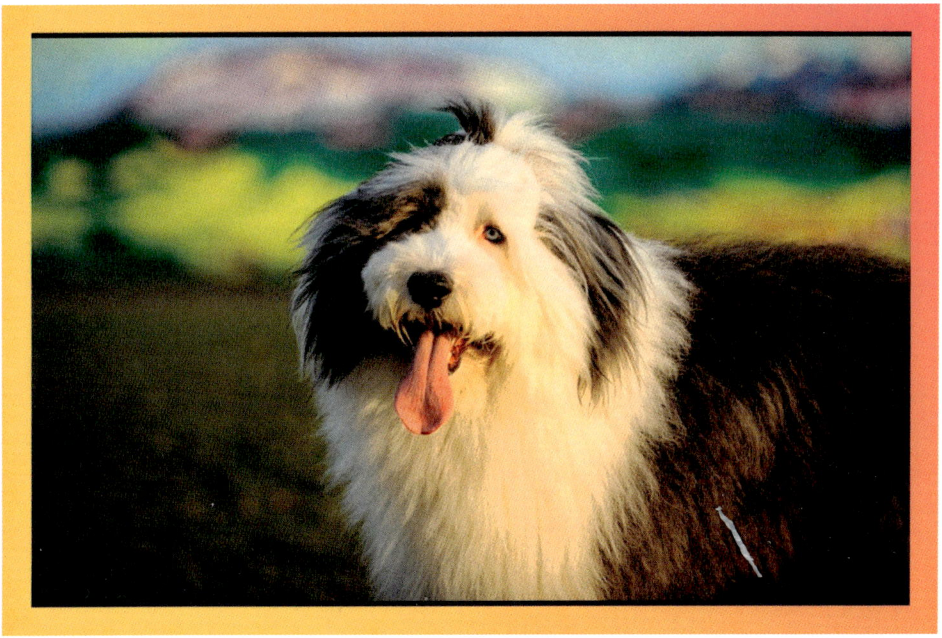

# In what year was these breed recognized?

Many years ago back in 1888, this dog breed was initially recognized. The breed was recognized by a kennel club.

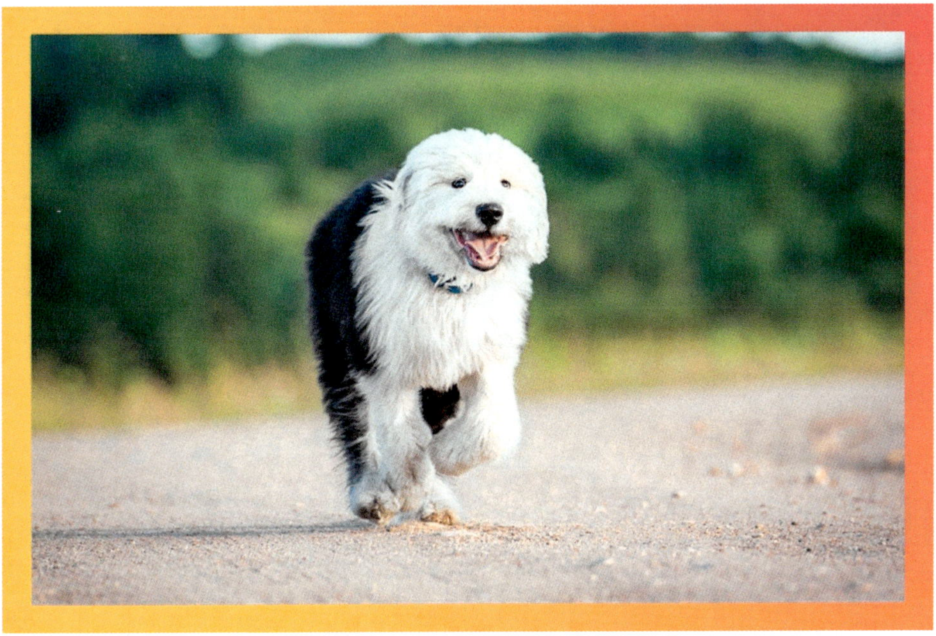

# How do people describe the Old English Sheepdog?

There are many words used to describe these dogs. Some people describe them as "big babies". They are also described as "loving and kind".

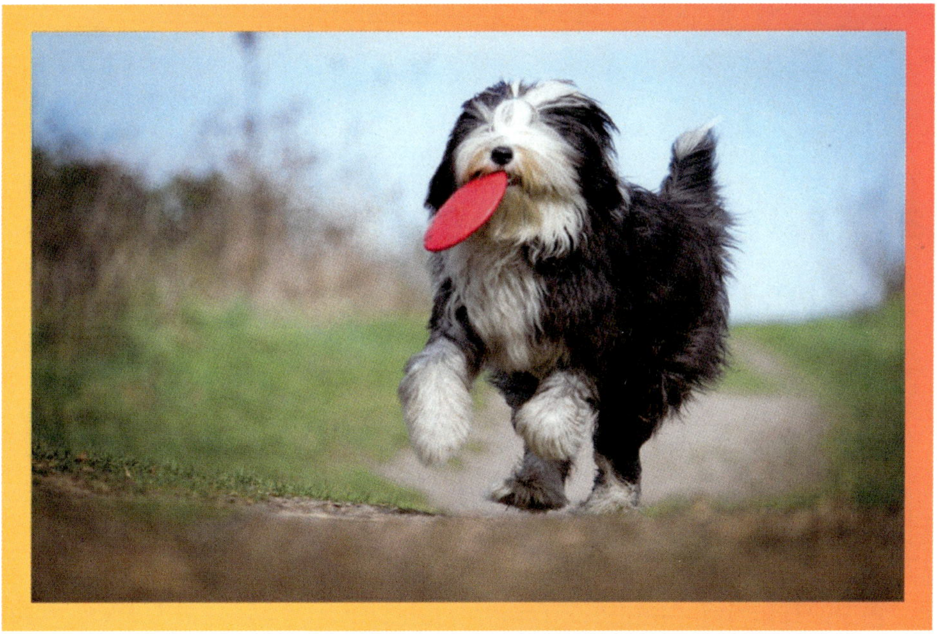

# Are these dogs a healthy breed?

The good news is that these dogs are a relatively healthy breed. They usually do not suffer from many health problems. Other dogs are prone to specific health problems, but fortunately, Old English Sheepdogs are quite healthy. They do, however, suffer from various eye problems and hearing problems, although this may only occur when they tend to get older.

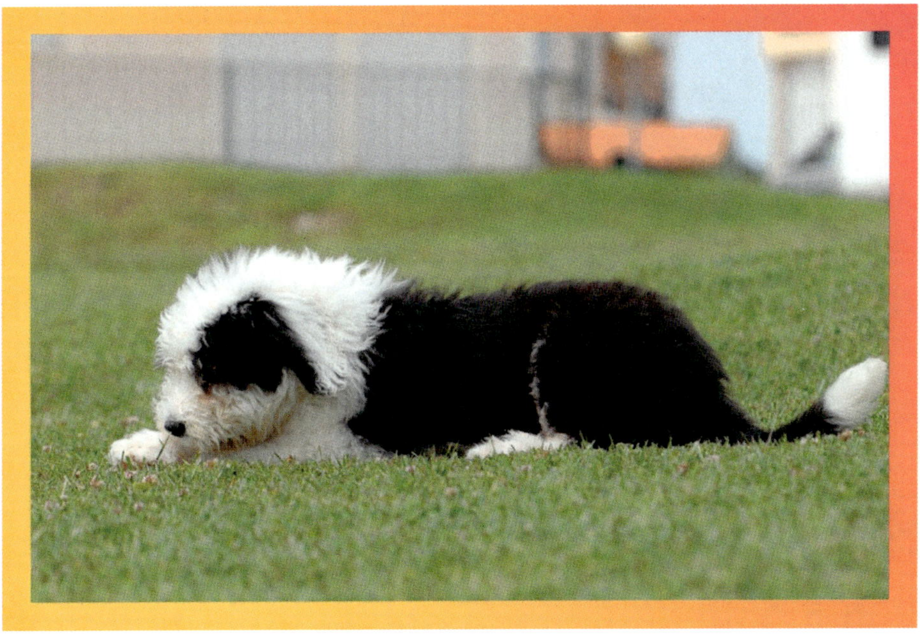

# Have famous people ever owned an Old English Sheepdog?

One of the most famous celebrities of all time, who was known for loving Old English Sheepdogs was none other than Beatles singer Paul McCartney. Paul and his girlfriend owned a beautiful Old English Sheepdog named Martha.

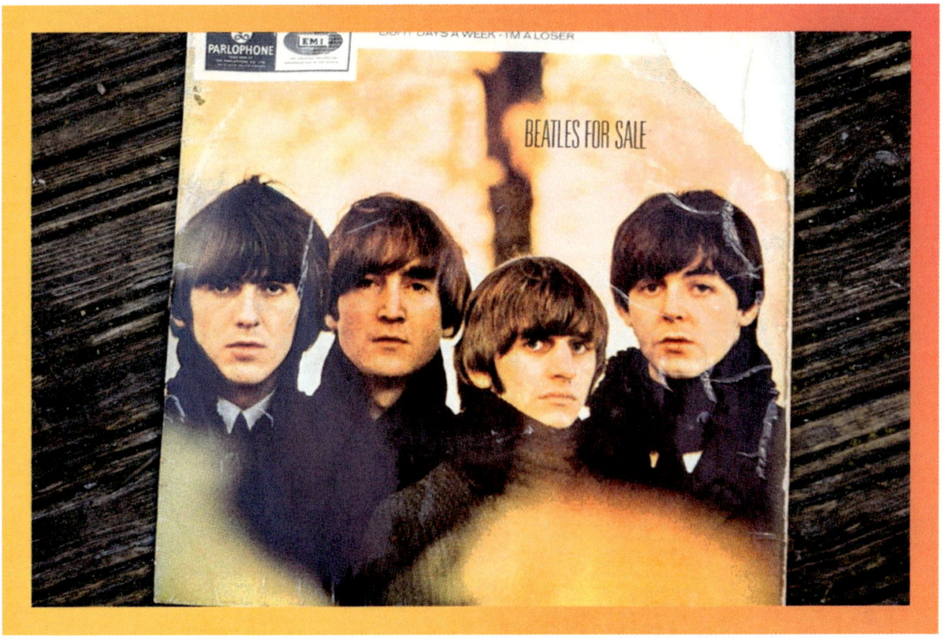
PARLOPHONE
EMI
BEATLES FOR SALE

# Has there ever been an Old English Sheepdog in a movie?

There have actually been made Old English Sheepdogs in the movies. Over the years many Old English Sheepdogs have appeared in all sorts of films. For example, they appeared in "101 Dalmations", "Chitty Chitty Bang Bang" and "12 Dogs of Christmas".

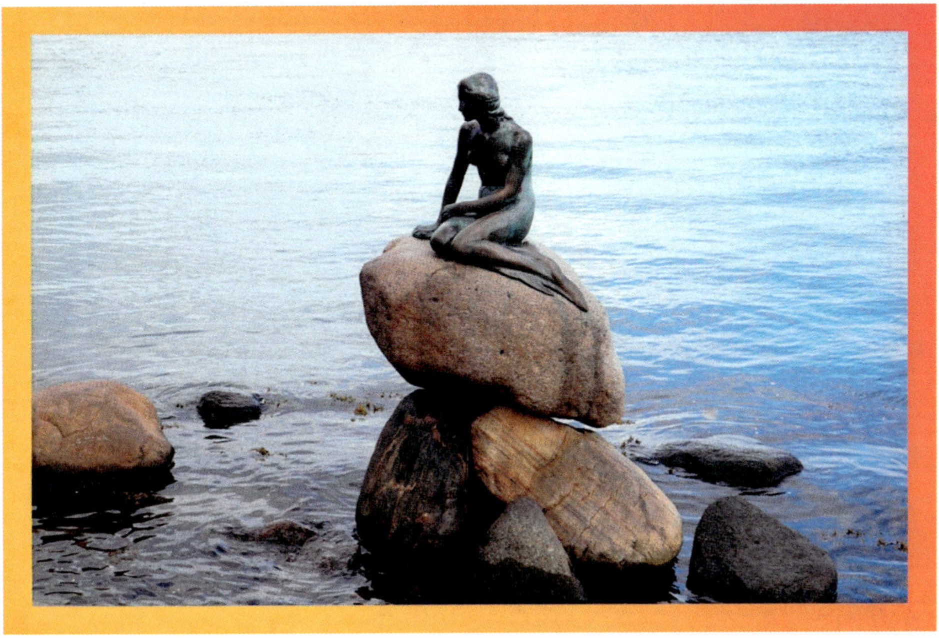

# Do Old English Sheepdogs make lots of noise?

Although these dogs do not make tons of noise, their bark is very loud. Their bark can become annoying to humans who are not used to the noise of constant dog barking.

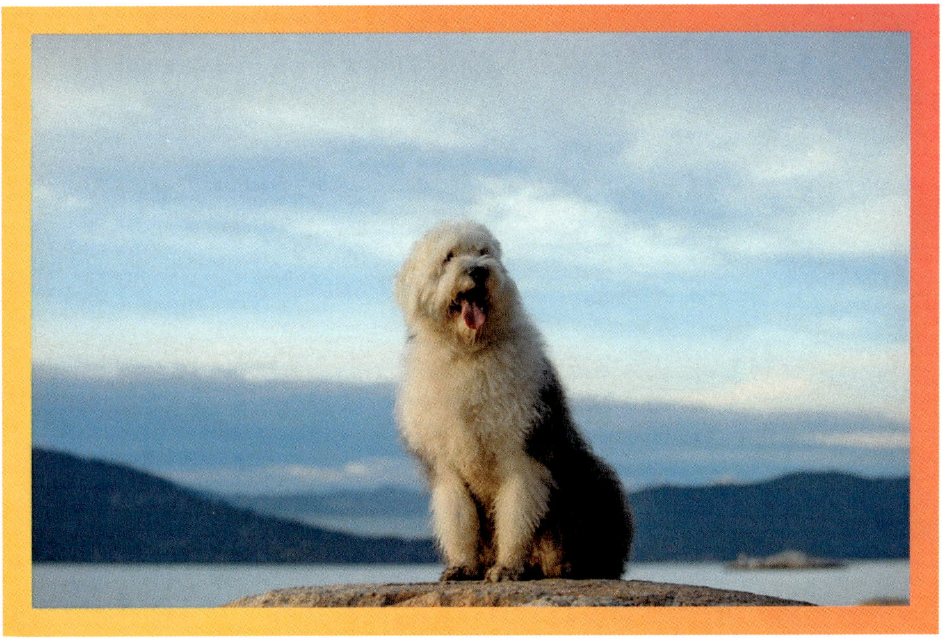

# How did the Old English Sheepdog breed become well- known in America?

Back in the days, these dogs were used by farmers. However, a couple of years later the upper-class American people found out about these dogs. Once they discovered this wonderful breed, it became a very popular choice amongst rich families in America.

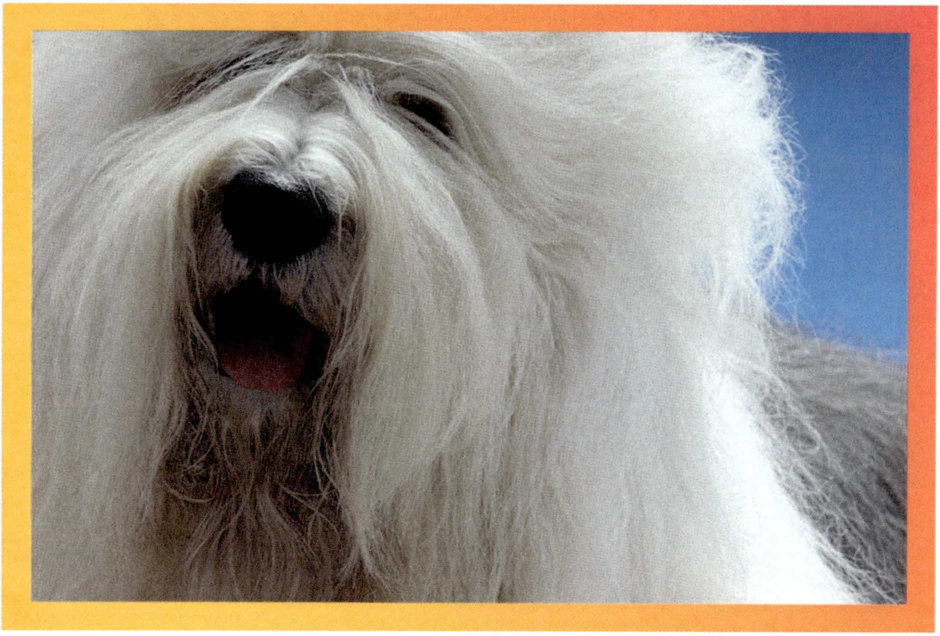

# Do these dogs need regular attention?

The answer is yes. Old English Sheepdogs require vast amounts of attention. They do not cope well being alone. They function best around other humans and animals. If you own one of these dogs you will need to pay your dog regular attention every single day.

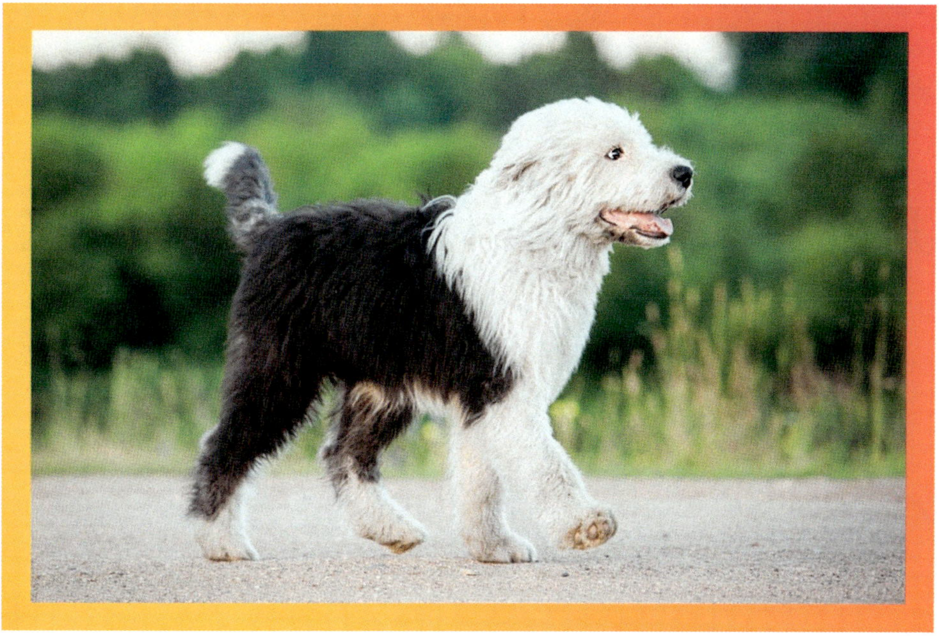

# Are Old English Sheepdogs very clean?

The answer is a big no. Old English Sheepdogs are prone to getting dirty all the time. Their thick coat attracts dirt and often drags on the ground. They also tend to drool a lot and get hot because of their coat. They can get extremely dirty and they are certainly not the cleanest of dog breeds.

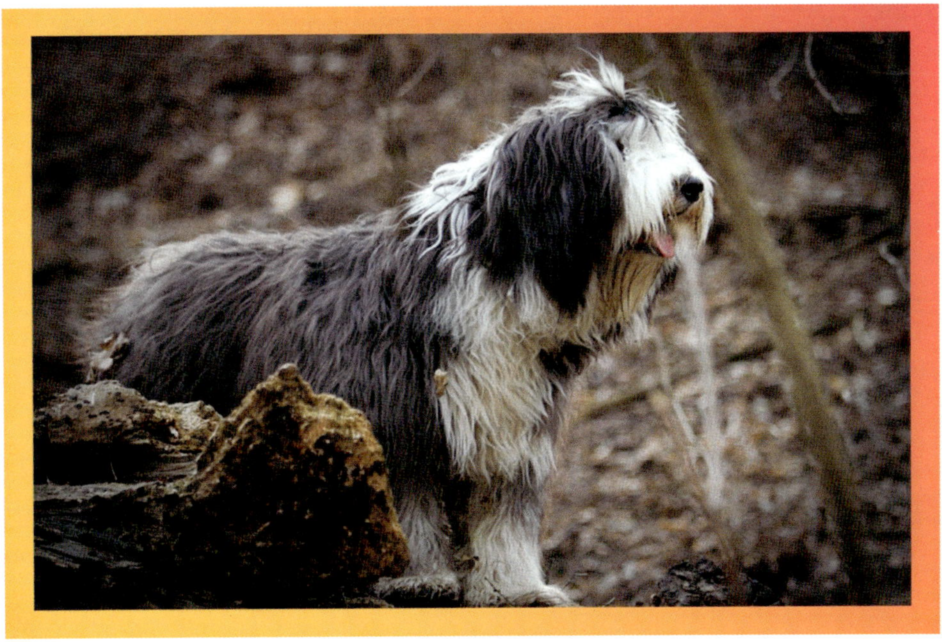

# What kind of lifespan do these dogs have?

The Old English sheepdog breed has an average lifespan of around 10 to 12 years. This is quite young in comparison to other dogs who can live to over 15 years of age.

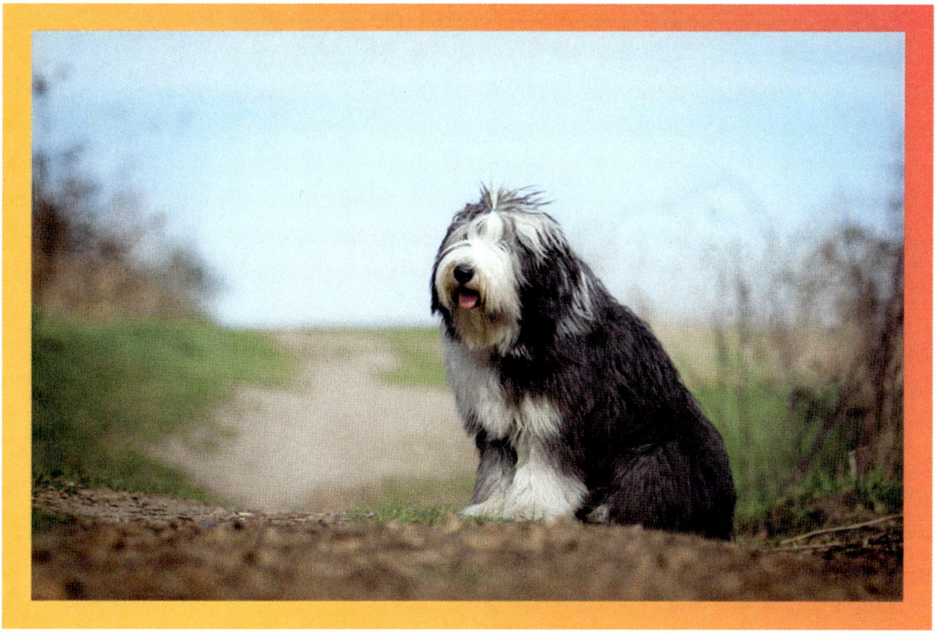

# Are there any nicknames given to Old English Sheepdogs?

Many years ago farmers started to dock their tails. This was used as a method to prove that their dogs were used for working purposes. They did this in order to try to obtain tax exceptions from the government. This is how the nickname "bobtail" came about.

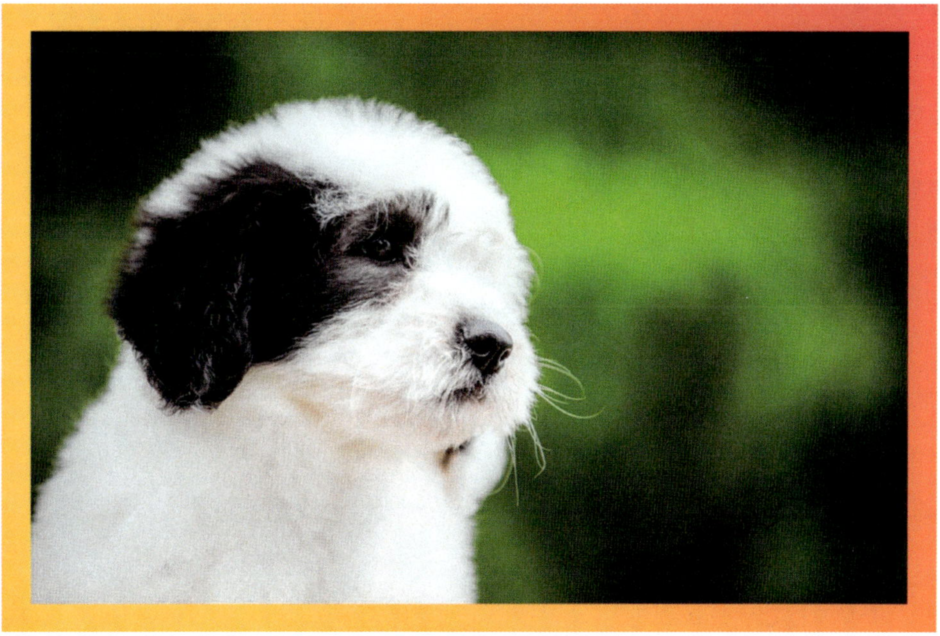

# Do Old English Sheepdogs need to be groomed often?

The answer is yes. These dogs have a very thick coat and they are prone to getting dirty very quickly. If you own an Old English Sheepdog you will need to be prepared to spend a couple of hours every single week grooming your dog.

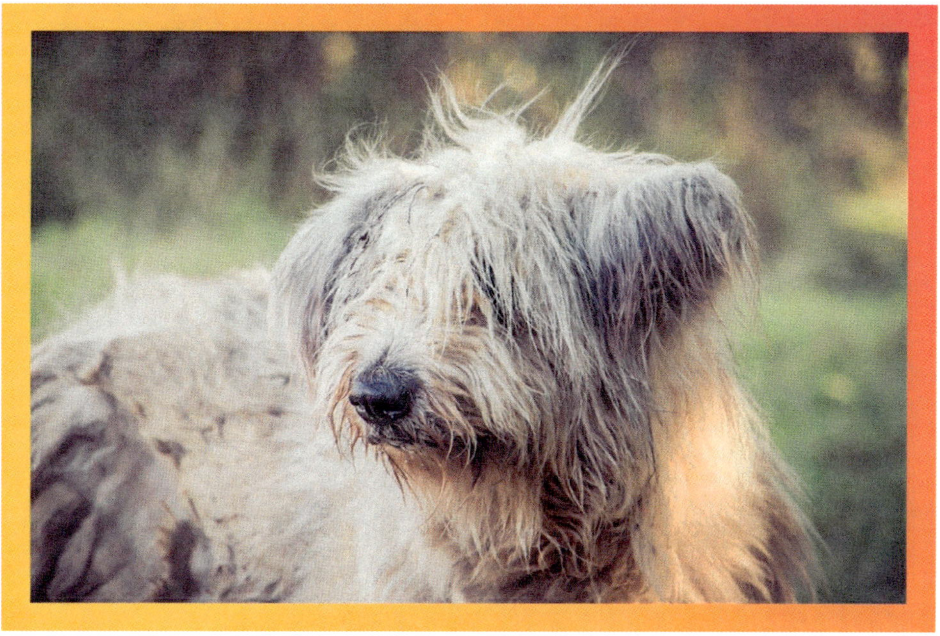

# What type of coat does the Old English Sheepdog have?

These dogs are known for their exceptionally thick coat. Their coat makes them ideal for herding sheep as they can keep warm in cold weather conditions.

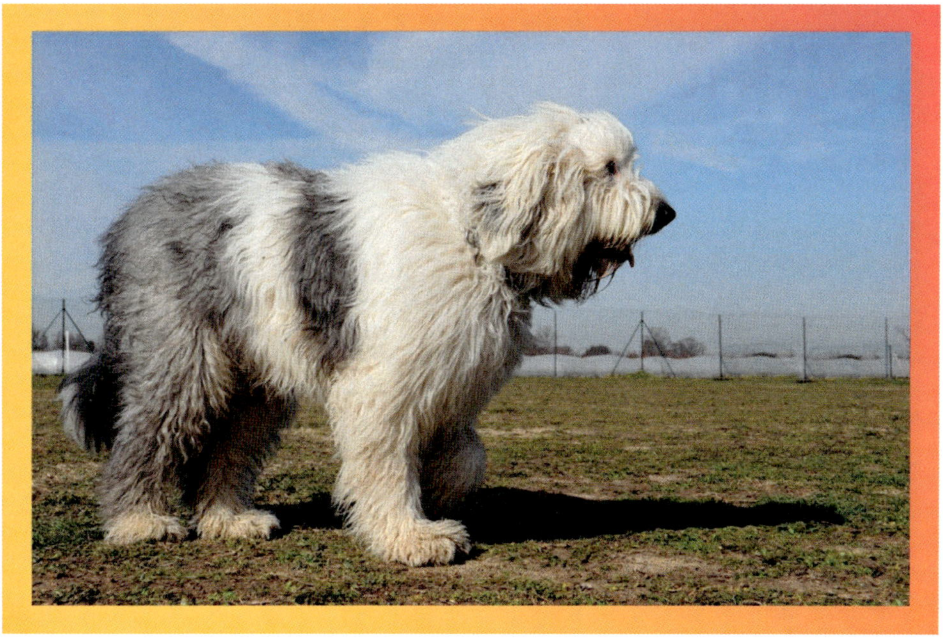

# How big are Old English Sheepdogs?

In terms of heights Old English Sheep Dogs, females range from 51-56 cm. The males range from 56-61 cm in height. In terms of weight, the females weigh anything from 27-36 kg and the males weigh around 32-45kg.

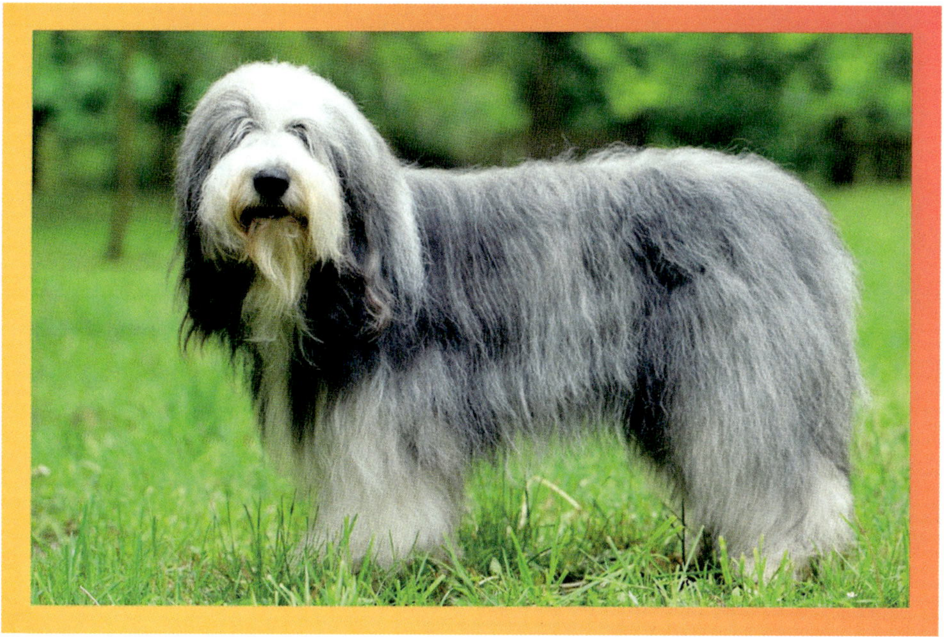

# Which type of dogs do these dogs belong to?

Old English Sheepdogs belong to the breed of herding dogs. These dogs were all bred in order to herd animals.

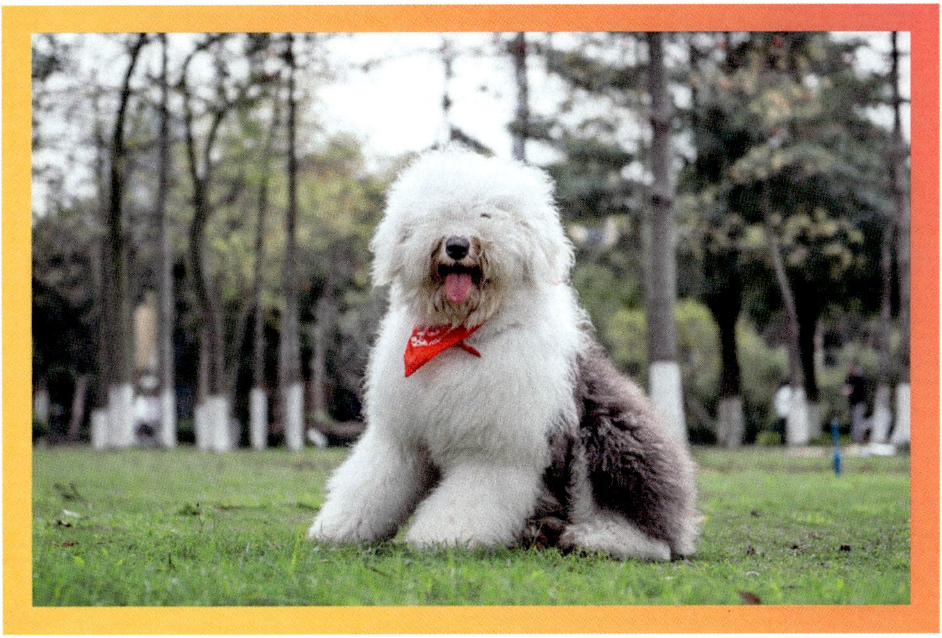

# What were Old English Sheepdogs bred for?

These dogs were bred specifically in order to herd sheep. They were also bred in order to herd cattle.

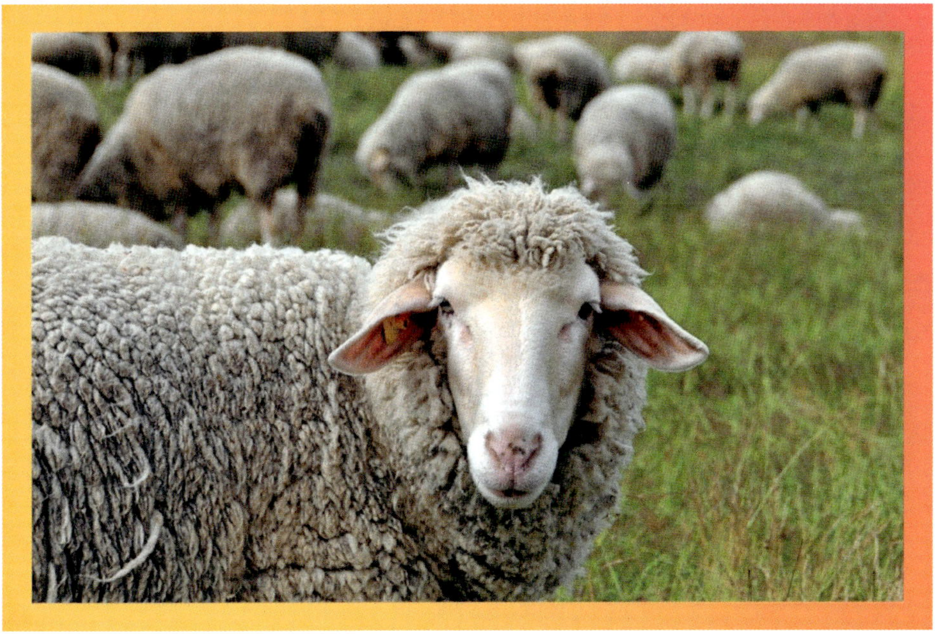

# Are Old English Sheepdogs old dogs?

Don't be fooled by their name. The truth is that these dogs are actually relatively young in comparison to other dog breeds. They have only been around for around 150 years.

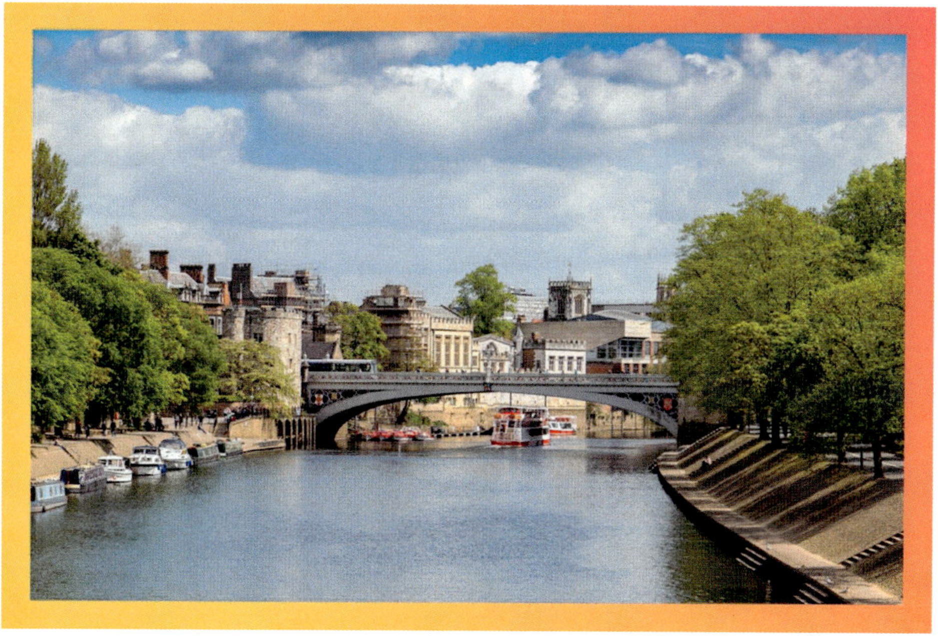

Made in the USA
Monee, IL
25 March 2021